D0319211

To Anna and Owen – C.L.
For Todd and all his friends in Miss Perryman's class – A.W.

First published in Great Britain in 1999 by Macdonald Young Books

Macdonald Young Books
an imprint of Wayland Publishers Ltd
61 Western Road
Hove
East Sussex
BN3 1JD

You can find Macdonald Young Books on the internet at:
http://www.myb.co.uk

Commissioning Editor Dereen Taylor
Editor Rosie Nixon
Designer Liz Black
Science and Language Consultant Dr Carol Ballard

Text © Claire Llewellyn 1999
Illustrations © Amanda Wood 1999
Volume © Macdonald Young Books 1999
M.Y.Bees artwork © Clare Mackie

All rights reserved. No part of this book may be reproduced, stored in a retrieval system or transmitted by any other
means, electronic, mechanical, photocopying or otherwise, without the prior permission of the Publisher.

Claire Llewellyn
Paint a Sun in the Sky: a first look at seasons.
(MYBees)
1. Seasons - Juvenile Literature
I. Title II. Wood, Amanda.
508.2

Printed and bound in Asa, Portugal

ISBN 0 7500 2788 6

Paint a Sun in the Sky

A first look at the seasons

Paint a Sun in the Sky

A first look at the seasons

by Claire Llewellyn

MACDONALD YOUNG BOOKS

In spring, the first buds open on the trees.

Mmm! The weather's getting warmer. It must be spring.

And it's still light when we get home from school.

Spring blossom opens, and flowers

shoot up through the chilly ground.

9

11

In summer, the sun is high in the sky.

Out go thick jumpers and heavy coats.

12

In come sunhats, T-shirts and shorts.

Flowerbeds and windowboxes buzz with bees.

Bees use nectar to make honey.

14

In early autumn, nuts, berries, apples

18

Soon, the leaves on the trees change colour

In winter, the sun is low in the sky.

The days are short and cold.

The best winter days have

bright sunshine and snow.

all winter long. They'll wake up again in the spring.

That squirrel looks warm and cosy!

Why do we have seasons?

We have seasons because of the way the Earth moves around the Sun. This journey is called the Earth's orbit and it takes exactly one year.

1 In December, the South Pole leans towards the Sun. The south has summer. The north has winter.

The Earth isn't upright as it orbits the Sun. It's tilted to one side. So, at different times on its journey, first one pole and then the other leans towards the Sun. This is why we have seasons.

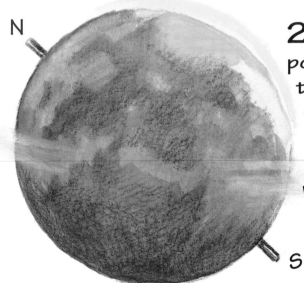

2 In March, neither pole leans towards the Sun, but the south is getting cooler (autumn) and the north is warming up (spring).

4 In September, neither pole leans towards the Sun, but it's getting warmer in the south (spring) and cooler in the north (autumn).

S

N

S

3 In June, the North Pole leans towards the Sun.
The north has summer.
The south has winter.

Useful words

Blossom
Small flowers that open on trees in spring.

Nectar
The sweet juice inside a flower.

Orbit
The pathway of the Earth as it moves around the Sun.

Pole
The name given to the most northern and most southern parts of the Earth.

Season
A part of the year that has its own sort of weather.

OTHER M.Y.Bees FOR YOU TO ENJOY:

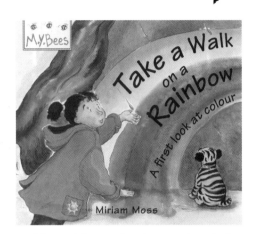

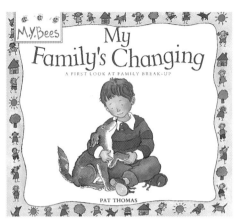

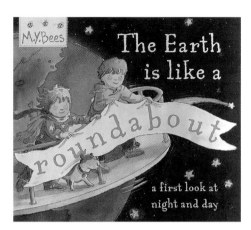

Take a Walk on a Rainbow – a first look
at colour
Miriam Moss
Illustrated by Amanda Wood
ISBN: 07500 2777 0

My Family's Changing – a first look
at family break-up
Pat Thomas
Illustrated by Lesley Harker
ISBN: 07500 2571 9

The Earth is like a Roundabout – a first look
at night and day
Claire Llewellyn
Illustrated by Anthony Lewis
ISBN: 07500 2644 8

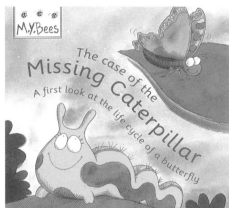

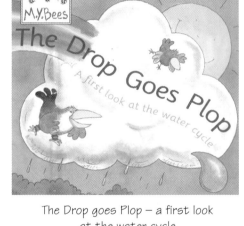

The Trouble with Tadpoles – a
first look at the life cycle of a frog
Sam Godwin
Illustrated by Simone Abel
ISBN: 07500 2652 9

The Case of the Missing Caterpillar – a first look
at the life cycle of a butterfly
Sam Godwin
Illustrated by Simone Abel
ISBN: 07500 2651 0

The Drop goes Plop – a first look
at the water cycle
Sam Godwin
Illustrated by Simone Abel
ISBN: 07500 2494 1

All these books and many more can be purchased from your local bookseller. For more information, write to:

The Sales Department   Macdonald Young Books   61 Western Road   Hove   BN3 1JD